RURAL RA

C000044492

In Sur...

Janet Spayne and Graham Mitchell-Gears

COUNTRYSIDE BOOKS

NEWBURY, BERKSHIRE

First published 2004
© Janet Spayne and Graham Mitchell-Gears 2004

COUNTRYSIDE BOOKS
3 Catherine Road
Newbury, Berkshire

ISBN 1 85306 831 4

Photographs by the authors
Designed by Graham Whiteman

Produced through MRM Associates Ltd., Reading
Typeset by Mac Style Ltd, Scarborough, N. Yorkshire
Printed by J. W. Arrowsmith Ltd., Bristol

Contents

AREA MAP SHOWING LOCATIONS OF THE WALKS

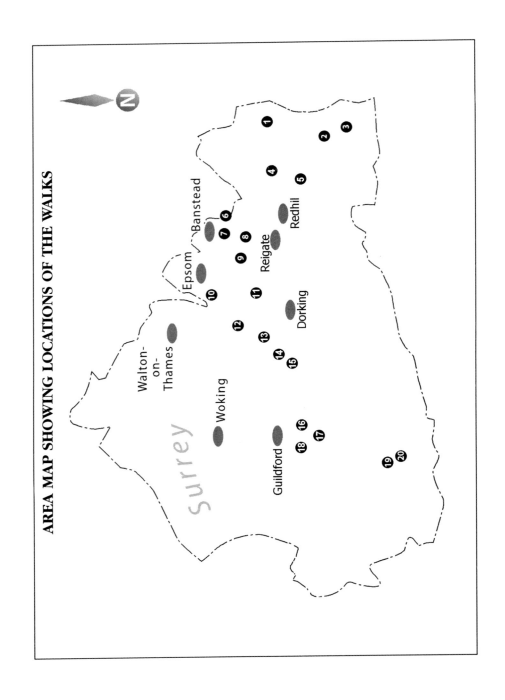

PUBLISHER'S NOTE

We hope that you obtain considerable enjoyment from this book; great care has been taken in its preparation. Although at the time of publication all routes followed public rights of way or permitted paths, diversion orders can be made and permissions withdrawn.

We cannot, of course, be held responsible for such diversion orders and any inaccuracies in the text which might result from these or any other changes to the routes nor any damage which might result from walkers trespassing on private property. We are anxious though that all details covering the walks are kept up to date and would therefore welcome information from readers which would be relevant to future editions.

The simple sketch maps that accompany the walks in this book are based on notes made by the authors whilst checking out the routes on the ground. They are designed to show you how to reach the start, to point out the main features of the overall circuit and they contain a progression of numbers that relate to the paragraphs of the text.

However, for the benefit of a proper map, we do recommend that you purchase the relevant Ordnance Survey sheet covering your walk. The Ordnance Survey maps are widely available, especially through booksellers and local newsagents.

INTRODUCTION

Many years ago, I co-wrote a book of walks with a friend, Audrey Krynski, based on the Surrey Hills. To my surprise and delight, it is still in print and has, in fact, been revised for another edition in 2004. Now, in collaboration with my son-in-law, Graham Mitchell-Gears, I have devised another selection of walks that I hope will entice you to put on your walking boots.

The county of Surrey is a delight for walking in any season and all the routes in this book are meant to be taken at a leisurely pace so that you can savour and enjoy the sights along the way.

Lingering along the hedgerows in winter, you may spot a cluster of hundreds of hibernating ladybirds nestled at the base of a shrub. When the hazel catkins appear during a warm spell early in the year, stop and seek for tiny red female flowers which will be the future nuts. Peer through hedges and you will be surprised at what you see – woodland carpeted with wild aconites near Leatherhead, or snowdrops at Shere. In woods and on heathland, there are plenty of deer to spot if you are quiet and, on warm days in spring, adders may be seen basking on the soil or bracken. Linger by the water to watch dragonflies and damselflies, possibly even a snake swimming. Kingfishers are not rare in Surrey, either.

And, of course, the downs are full of wildflowers – Surrey has one of the best collections of orchids in the country as they enjoy the chalky soil. Look out for the 'roses' on larch trees in spring, and in autumn the hedges are full of blackberries, sloes and hips: there may be mushrooms in the meadows, too.

Pass slowly through peaceful villages with numerous different types of building, many of them centuries old. The churches, in particular, are worth a peep inside if you have time. In fact, there is just so much to see on these walks that even a short circuit can stretch into a day, especially if you stop for something to eat along the way. Refreshment places are mentioned, though on some routes, a picnic might be an enjoyable option.

All the walks have been designed to explore the less frequented parts of Surrey, using quiet footpaths away from the hills, and none of them should be too taxing. Remember, though, that mud can be a common feature in the countryside, even in the drier months, so we do recommend that you wear some stout shoes or boots. An added bonus is that all the routes start from a railway station or bus stop, so you have the option of leaving the car at home.

Finally, as every season has its attractions, do try and repeat the walks at different times of the year. In that way, you will get the best out of the countryside.

Happy walking; and as William Henry Davies wrote:

> 'What is this life if, full of care,
> We have no time to stand and stare.'

Janet Spayne

OXTED AND LIMPSFIELD COMMON

❧

Along the route from Limpsfield

Here is a varied walk over fields and meadows and common land which is suitable for any time of the year. There are two wide stiles and one very short, fairly steep uphill stretch, but plenty of places to rest and admire the scenery. The sandy ground makes for good walking.

- **HOW TO GET THERE:** By train or bus to Oxted station.
- **PARKING:** There are several car parks in the vicinity.
- **LENGTH OF THE WALK:** 5 miles. Maps: OS Explorer 146 and 147 (GR 394528).

THE WALK

1. Leaving Oxted station from the downside platform we go down Station Approach to the main road where we turn right

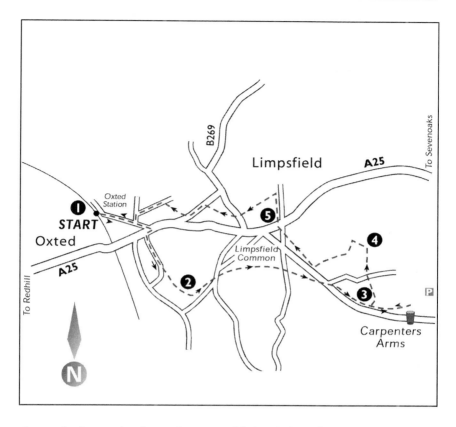

through the main shopping area. Maintaining direction up Snatts Hill we reach the A25 where we turn right to cross, by the traffic island, to walk up Uvedale Road, going gently uphill. At the top, just before the road bears right, we turn left on a fenced path between houses. This tarmac path goes steeply uphill to bring us to West Heath, a National Trust common. Coming to an open area there is a large house on the left and a log over to the right where we may sit for a rest.

2. Keeping on the common we maintain our original direction on a path parallel with the service road on the left. At a crossing track we continue straight ahead, eventually joining the service road where we turn right to a road. Crossing to a signposted footpath opposite we continue on Limpsfield Common, soon

11

reaching another road. We cross into a small car park opposite and turn left on a signposted footpath, following this pleasant footpath for about $\frac{1}{4}$ mile, ignoring all side turnings. At a road junction we cross two roads to take a signposted footpath opposite, soon with a golf course either side. We emerge at a small road and cross to the track opposite, bearing towards the main road. Crossing the main road we continue direction and, at some trees ahead, our path runs parallel with the main road. We cross a drive and come back to the main road. At a house on the right we turn left on a signposted bridleway.

3. If we want refreshment we continue along the main road for a few more yards and take a tarmac path on the left, going through trees to reach another road which we cross to a gravel road opposite. There are a few houses on the left and at the corner is the Carpenters Arms, a pub much frequented by ramblers. Opposite there is a National Trust common with a few seats for a picnic.

To continue our walk we go down the bridleway, passing a few houses, and at the end bear left into a sloping field. There are splendid views ahead to the North Downs. At the bottom of the field we cross a road to a gate opposite, walking towards a small copse. There is a waymarked post on the corner and we turn left with the copse on our right.

4. Bearing right at the end of the copse we then turn left on a path towards a hedge. At the hedge we turn left, keeping it on our right, and at the end of this crop field go over a wide stile into open woodland, bearing right. The track eventually reaches the golf course and we continue along the edge. At the corner we turn right into a wide bridleway and take the right hand of two tracks, which brings us to the Club House and a National Trust car park.

5. We cross the A25 to the National Trust sign opposite and continue along the edge of more golf course, with the hedge on our right. At the last green there is a log on which we might rest. Looking out for golfers, we cross the green to trees opposite,

There are plenty of wide open spaces on this walk where you can admire the view

making for a gap to the left of a white notice. Entering woodland we ignore a right fork and drop gently downhill, eventually reaching Limpsfield High Street where we cross the road and turn right. Very soon we turn left on a signposted drive taking us through a waymarked gate into Padbrook. Following the main roadway we reach another road where we turn left. Crossing the road we soon take a signposted footpath between houses, go over a stile and into a meadow. Going diagonally left across the field we pass through a barrier in the far corner. The path now becomes enclosed and finally reaches a residential road where we turn left. At the next junction we turn left and go downhill, passing the library, to the main street of Oxted. We turn right, and cross on the pedestrian crossing, soon reaching the station.

Refreshments: The Carpenters Arms at Limpsfield Chart, and a variety at Oxted.

WALK 2

SOUTH GODSTONE AND CROWHURST

Mansion House, Crowhurst

This is a pleasant walk through farmland and woodland, giving us the chance to see the ancient yew tree in Crowhurst churchyard. In autumn, there are sloes and blackberries in the hedgerows, but this is a good walk for any time of the year, though there are plenty of stiles to negotiate.

- **HOW TO GET THERE:** By train or bus to South Godstone station.
- **PARKING:** At the railway station.
- **LENGTH OF THE WALK:** 5 miles. Map: OS Explorer 146 (GR 362483).

THE WALK

1. Leaving the station by the approach road we turn right at the main road to go under the railway bridge. Immediately

14

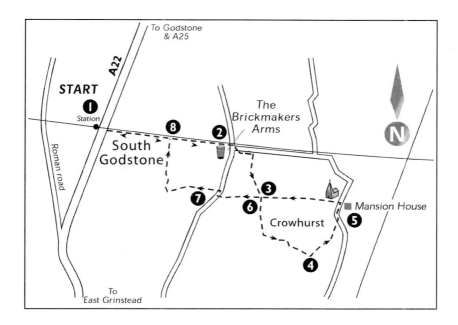

under the bridge we cross the road with care to a signposted footpath opposite, going over a stile into a meadow. We follow this path for almost a mile, alongside the railway, going through a number of fields with pleasant aspects and crossing several stiles.

2. Emerging at the Brickmakers Arms we cross the road to a small residential road opposite. It is worth turning to look back at this attractive old inn – in summer bright with hanging baskets. After about 300 yards along this little road we look for a narrow turning on the right, beside a bungalow, with a concrete footpath sign, and follow this enclosed footpath between houses. The path continues to be enclosed across two fields then we go over a bridge and gently uphill, with woods over to the left, gradually bearing left. At the top of the field, by a fence, we turn left, over a stile, into woods.

3. In a few yards we turn right and follow a narrow path through trees, passing a small pond on the right, eventually

15

reaching a stile into a field. We go diagonally across this field, to the far left hand corner, through a gate and ahead through farm buildings. At the end of the buildings we go through a gate on the left onto a tarmac farm track. We follow this track and when it bears left, we turn right on a private road for a few yards. At a large tree on the right, with a footpath sign on it, we go diagonally left across a large field, making for a bridge in the hedge ahead. The path is not always visible, especially after ploughing, but if we aim for the tall chimney, on the skyline, we will not be far out.

4. Once over the bridge we turn left, with a plantation of young trees on the right at the end of which we cross a stile into another field. In a few yards we turn left, over another stile, to go over another bridge. We bear diagonally right to a stile, in a fence, and continue direction to yet another stile, in the corner of the field, taking us into a narrow track. Turning right we reach the road where we turn left uphill to Crowhurst church.

The church is about 700 years old and the ancient yew, by the east window, is reputedly 1,400 years old, and still flourishing. The church is locked but the notice board gives telephone numbers of several officials and it might be possible to get a key. There is a seat by the lychgate. Opposite the church is the attractive Mansion House, a late medieval house with a 17th century front.

5. With the lychgate behind us and with the church on our right, a path takes us to a gate into a rough field where we continue along the top edge. At the end of this field another stile takes us into a chalk track (which can be very slippery after rain) and, maintaining direction, we soon go through woods, eventually coming to a stile we crossed earlier.

6. Here we take the left hand of two stiles and go gently downhill, with a fence over to the right. At a fence across the field there are two stiles, one by the right hand fence and one more to the left, which is the one we want. Bearing slightly left, we go gently downhill, to a stile in the hedge leading to a bridge

The ancient yew at Crowhurst is reputed to be 1,400 years old

over a stream. After crossing the bridge we turn left alongside a lake and right up to a gate and stile to a road where we turn right.

7. After a few yards, by the side of a house, we turn left on a signposted bridleway, passing a few houses. Going through a gate we pass a house on the right, usually with some guard dogs in attendance, and continue forward to a gate taking us into a hedged lane, which soon gives way to open crop fields. In just under $^1/_2$ mile the track turns right, soon reaching a crossing track where we turn right. After about 150 yards this wide footpath turns sharply right and we keep straight ahead, on a grassy path with the fence on our left at first, towards a red brick railway bridge visible ahead.

8. At the bridge we turn left, and retrace our steps parallel with the railway, back to the road, under the railway bridge and back to the station.

Refreshments: The Brickmakers Arms, and also at South Godstone.

WALK 3

LINGFIELD

Eden Brook

We start this walk by exploring some of the older parts of Lingfield with many houses from the 16th to 18th centuries. We pass the 500 year old church of St Peter and St Paul, and the village lock-up last used in 1882. The walk then passes through farm fields with wide open aspects and crosses the Meridian Line twice where there are stones placed to commemorate the Millennium.

- **HOW TO GET THERE:** By train to Lingfield station.
- **PARKING:** At the railway station.
- **LENGTH OF THE WALK:** $5^1/_2$ miles. Map: OS Explorer 146 (GR 395438).

THE WALK

1. Leaving the station by the approach road we cross the main road and take the tarmac footpath opposite with a stone

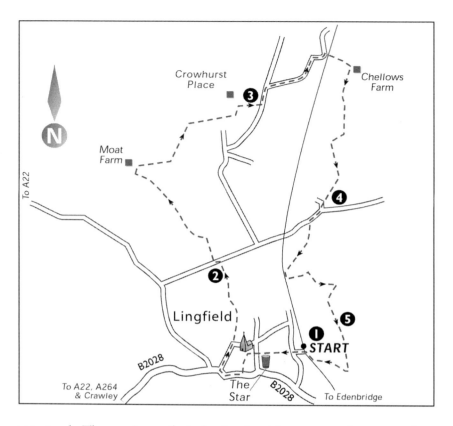

waymark. The main path is hedged with roses and we reach a small road at the side of The Star. We cross to a small drive between fine old houses leading to the church. Entering the churchyard we fork left then left again to an enclosed footpath soon coming out to the main road, the B2028, where we turn right through the shopping centre. As the road bends left we maintain direction on a pedestrian path, soon with pretty garden seats and a pond on the left and the village cage next to an ancient hollow tree. From the cage we turn right up Vicarage Road and when the road turns sharply right we take the second of two signposted footpaths on the left. As the tarmac path turns sharply right we go slightly left onto a gravel path, taking the second smaller turning through a gap in the hedge on the left. Keeping the hedge on our right we go through a gap at the end of the field and fork left to go down to a gate and a drive. We turn right and soon right again to go over a stile and across a field to another stile in the corner, over which we turn left along an enclosed path to the road.

2. At the road we turn left and soon right on a signposted drive to Sugham Farm. Passing a pond on our left we keep the gravel drive and farm buildings on our left, soon joining an enclosed path and shortly turning right to go over a gated bridge. Maintaining direction across a field we go through a gap in the hedge to our right and bear left up to a stile. Crossing this field to a stile in the far corner we continue along a grassy ride and soon, opposite a stile in the fence on our left, go over a stile in the right hand hedge and turn right into the drive of Moat Farm. We go over a bridge and as the drive goes ahead we turn right onto a rutted cart track. After about 350 yards we turn left over a stile into a field, following the hedge on the left. At the next field we go slightly right up to a yellow waymarked post in the hedge ahead where we turn right along the edge of the field. We cross another stile and the orchard of Crowhurst Place is behind the hedge on our left. At a small wood we turn left to go through a gate and follow a wide grassy path with the wood on our right. The chimneys of Crowhurst Place are just visible on the left. Just beyond the trees the path continues ahead but we turn right to a stile into a field which we cross, with trees on the right, to a stile in the far corner, taking us into the road.

3. Turning left we pass the gatehouse of Crowhurst Place and very soon turn right on Pikes Lane, signposted to Oxted and Limpsfield. The road turns left and then right and at the next sharp left hand turn we go right up a rough road over the railway.

Passing a few houses and just before the farm buildings of Chellows Farm we turn right over a stile into a small field, crossing it to another stile into a large field. With a willow in a dip (crater) on the right we make for a solitary oak tree and go over the stile just beyond it. Crossing the waymarked stile to the left of the wood ahead we continue straight across this next field, making for a stile to the left of three large trees in the hedge. Immediately we turn right with the hedge on our right and just here there is a stone marking the Meridian Line, put there by the local councils, to mark the Millennium. At a gap ahead we bear left across the field on a signposted footpath to a stile in the corner. Maintaining direction over the next field we cross a stile in the corner. Turning right and keeping a hedge on our right we go through two fields to reach a small road.

4. Turning left for a few yards to a more major road we turn right (this is a very hazardous junction) and immediately after going over a river bridge turn left on a wide track. After a few yards we go over a stile on the left and bear right along the field, keeping the houses and hedge on our right. Continuing through various gates we eventually bear left alongside the railway and soon, by a ramp up to the railway line, turn left across the field to a stile. We maintain direction to cross a footbridge and, turning immediately right, soon reach a stile in the corner of the field which takes us along the next field with the hedge on our right. Crossing a stile we then turn right to cross another stile to bring us into a grassy track, later turning into a gravel drive. Continuing on a joining track and ignoring tracks to the left and right we take an enclosed track with a brick wall on our right.

5. When the track turns left, by a bungalow, we maintain direction across fields, eventually going through a gap in the hedge and turning right with a fence on our left. We go through a gate and forward over a footbridge, maintaining direction over another footbridge to bring us to the railway line, which we cross. We turn right to go either along the platform or along the track back to the car park.

Refreshments: The Star, also other options in Lingfield.

GODSTONE AND BLETCHINGLEY

Brewer Street

This interesting walk wanders through two of Surrey's oldest villages with many attractive houses and inns. We pass a working sand quarry, and then have the chance of a worthwile diversion to Bletchingley's Castle Hill where we can rest to enjoy the splendid view.

- **HOW TO GET THERE:** By bus to Godstone Green.
- **PARKING:** There is very restricted parking in the village.
- **LENGTH OF THE WALK:** 5 miles. Map: OS Explorer 146 (GR 350515).

THE WALK

1. Starting from the White Hart we cross the main road onto the village green, keeping the pond on our left and another road on our right. We cross the A25 to the Hare and Hounds and take a

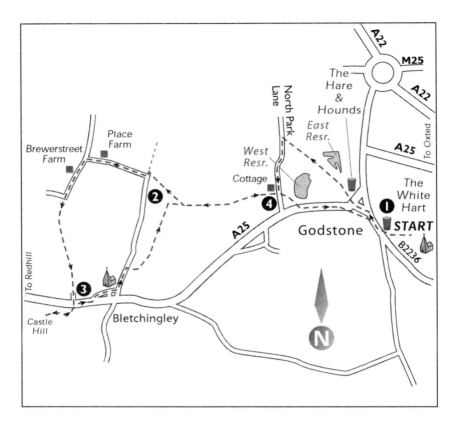

signposted footpath with the pub, toilets and a telephone box on our right. Soon a kissing gate, on the left, takes us into a sloping meadow, which we cross diagonally to another kissing gate leading into an enclosed path, with reservoirs either side. At the end of this path a stile takes us into a field which we cross diagonally towards a hedge and another stile with North Park Farm over to the right. We turn left in this narrow lane for about $^1/_4$ mile and at a gate on the right we may watch the conveyor belt carrying sand across the hillside and under the lane. At a cottage on the right we turn right on a bridleway and soon left on a wide sandy track which we follow for rather more than $^1/_2$ mile.

2. When we reach a small road we turn right and later pass Place Farm, which belonged to Anne of Cleves. There is not

The splendid view from Castle Hill

much of the original house left except the partially blocked front arch. At the T-junction we turn left down Brewer Street to pass the very attractive Brewerstreet Farm dating back to the 15th century. When the road bends to the right at a telephone box we continue straight ahead on a signposted footpath which rises gently for about $^1/_2$ mile. On reaching a small road we take the left hand path rising above it, eventually coming out to the main road at Bletchingley, where we turn left.

3. For a worthwhile diversion and a splendid viewpoint, when we reach Bletchingley we cross the road to a small road opposite and then take a footpath on the right going round Castle Hill. Part of the way along there is a large tree trunk where we may sit to enjoy the view before retracing our steps to the main street of Bletchingley.

Bletchingley has a very wide main street and many 14th, 15th and 16th century houses and inns encouraging us to dawdle through the village.

To resume the walk we continue along the main road and, at the war memorial, fork left on a narrow path, with more beautiful houses, to the church where there is a seat.

Ancient houses line the streets of Bletchingley

St Mary's church is mostly 11th century with some 13th and 15th century alterations and is well worth a visit.

We go through the churchyard and at the road turn left for a short distance to turn right on a signposted footpath through the golf course. The path across the golf course is well signposted, and will take us through the remains of an orchard, and later through a small strip of open woodland. We leave the golf course by a stile on the left and turning right we retrace part of the walk we were on earlier.

4. When we reach the cottage we turn left for a few yards to take a footpath on the right, going underneath the conveyor belt and we can stop to watch the sand being fed into the lorries. This path will bring us to the main road where we turn left until we reach the Hare and Hounds and the bus stop.

If we wish to visit Godstone church we turn down beside the White Hart and continue alongside Bay Pond, crossing the road and up steps to the church. Walker Miles, a pioneer of rambling clubs, is buried in the churchyard and his grave is marked by a sarsen stone. Next to the church is a group of old looking almshouses, in fact built in the 19th century, where there is a small chapel which is open to visitors for quiet meditation.

Refreshments: There are several inns at both Godstone and Bletchingley.

SOUTH NUTFIELD AND OUTWOOD

This attractive barn and pond can be seen near the park, South Nutfield

This gentle walk, with just a few stiles, takes us through a variety of fields and some woodland below the hills. We can enjoy pleasant open aspects and no steep gradients.

- **HOW TO GET THERE:** By train to South Nutfield station.
- **PARKING:** On Outwood Common. The car park is down the unsigned gravel track at the three-armed signpost by Outwood Mill (GR 326457).
- **LENGTH OF THE WALK:** $5^1/_4$ or $7^3/_4$ miles; Outwood circular $6^1/_2$ miles. Map: OS Explorer 146 (GR 305492).

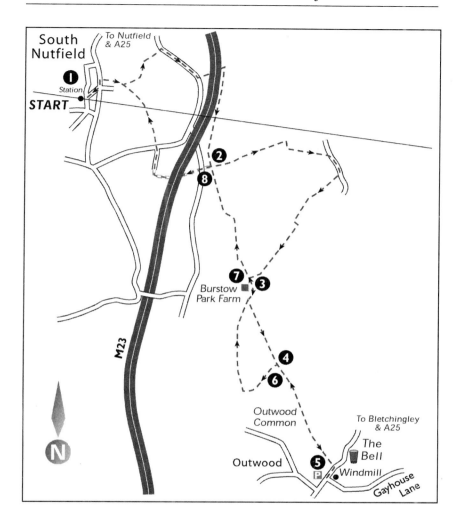

THE WALK

1. Leaving the north side (towards Tonbridge) platform of the station by the approach road takes us down to the main road where we turn left and very shortly right on a signposted footpath. This gravel track behind houses leads us over a stile into a large field. With the hedge on our left we go through a gap in the corner of the field and continue with the hedge now on our right. Going over a double stile we turn left up the

29

field to a stile then diagonally across the next field and out to a road where we turn right. After about 400 yards we turn left on a signposted footpath and continue under the motorway. At the end of the concrete drive we turn right over a stile and keeping this hedge on our right we later go over the railway. When this hedge finally ends we bear slightly left and at a farm road we turn left.

2. Following this farm road for just over $^3/_4$ mile we reach a road and, turning right, we soon turn right again to enter Bransland Wood, at a small National Trust car park. This is an attractive little wood with a pond and seat, with bluebells and primroses in spring. We take the main path downhill through an avenue of Wellingtonia to a gate taking us into a field.

We bear right and follow the field boundary passing, at the end of the field, a gate on the right leading to Access Land where we may picnic. Following the field round we turn right through a gap in the hedge into a field and maintain direction through gaps visible ahead towards a house, Burstow Park Farm. For the shorter walk from South Nutfield, we go over a waymarked stile on the right and continue the walk from **7.**

3. For the longer walk we turn left through a waymarked gate and right, round the edge of a small field with the attractive farmhouse on our right. Going through a gate we continue down to a main track, turn right, and at a signpost and a junction of paths we turn left on the footpath (the others are bridleways) with a hedge on the right. After going through a gate we go through the middle of the next, large field, then over a stile into another large field. We cross this field to reach a wide stile with a large tree either side. If we do not wish to go to Outwood Windmill we turn right with the hedge on our left and continue the walk from **6.**

4. For the extension to Outwood Mill we cross the stile and continue direction on a wide path along the side of the field with a hedge on the left. Passing a wide turning on the right we bear very slightly left over the next field, close to some large

The 17th century Outwood Mill is the oldest working mill in England

trees on the right, to a stile visible ahead. A small path takes us to a tarmac drive which we follow to the road, passing a few houses. (For return to the car park we turn right over the green to the gravel track.) The windmill is just ahead and the Bell Inn is a short distance to the left. Outwood Mill was built in 1665 and is the oldest working mill in England.

5. From the three-armed signpost opposite the windmill, we take the Bletchingley road with the mill on our right, in a few yards turning left on a signposted tarmac lane toward some houses. The lane ends in a small footpath going down to a stile which we cross into a field. We bear slightly left towards some large trees keeping them on our left, passing a turning on the left at the end of the trees. We maintain direction through a large field with a hedge on our right to a wide stile with a large tree either side. Crossing the stile we turn left with the hedge on our left.

6. We go slightly downhill to a stile taking us through a strip of woodland and over a small stream, up to another stile into a field.

Keeping straight on, with the hedge on our left, we reach another stile into a wide bridleway where we turn right. Continuing on this bridleway for some distance we eventually go through a gap in the hedge before Burstow Park Farm. Crossing a farm track slightly right to a gate we turn left at the signpost up to another gate and continue through a small field with the farmhouse on our left. At the end we turn right to leave the field by a gate in the hedge and we cross diagonally left to a waymarked stile.

7. Crossing this small field slightly left we go over a stile ahead and turn left shortly over another stile then turn right to follow the hedge to a bridge over a stream. Bearing left we cross the corner of a field to a stile ahead, bearing left again to cross another stile and continue up the side of the field with a hedge on our right. Just before a fence crossing the field, we fork left to a waymarked stile in the fence and go very gently uphill towards another stile. A plank bridge and stile take us into an enclosed footpath with a small pond and an attractive barn on the right. A stile takes us into a surfaced drive where we turn left up to a farm road.

8. To return to Outwood Mill, turn right on the farm road and follow the walk from **2. To continue to South Nutfield station**, turn left on the farm track to reach the road which we cross to a signposted footpath. Passing round behind stables we continue with the hedge on our right and fine views on our left. Going through a gap in the hedge ahead we soon bear right into the hedge and after crossing the motorway we reach a small car parking area where we turn right. This drive takes us past a field with llamas and out to the road where we turn left and shortly right on a signposted footpath into a Woodland Trust wood. Soon we bear left onto a gravel track and in the field corner keep left to go up over the railway. After a stile we keep the hedge on our left, cross a plank bridge then bear left across the next field to a stile by a gate. This gravelly track takes us back to the road where we turn left for the railway station.

Refreshments: Shops at South Nutfield. The Bell Inn at Outwood.

CHIPSTEAD: PARK DOWNS AND BANSTEAD WOOD

Stitchwort and bluebells line the track through Banstead Wood in spring

This splendid walk along downland is good at any time of year. The many berried hedgerow shrubs and marvellous views across to colourful woodland make it a delight in autumn. In spring there will be cowslips and bluebells, and in summer the downland will be ablaze with flowers.

- **HOW TO GET THERE:** By train to Chipstead station, then go down Station Approach and turn left on the main road, crossing to a gate on the right. Go along a strip of grassland to arrive at the car park. By bus, alight at the Midday Sun in Chipstead Valley Road and walk along the road for just over $^{1}/_{2}$ mile to the car park.

- **PARKING:** Banstead Wood car park in Holly Lane.
- **LENGTH OF THE WALK:** 5 miles. Map: OS Explorer 146 (Chipstead station GR 277583).

THE WALK

1. From the car park we cross two roads and turn left for a few yards to take the second signposted footpath going uphill with woods on the right and open hillside on the left. Passing a waymark we bear left then immediately fork right into a 'tunnel' of trees, following this twisting path uphill to a crossing track and waymarked post. Turning left we continue along the contour for about $^1/_4$ mile when we reach a 30 mph sign at the road. We cross to a footpath opposite and continue direction. At a junction of paths we make for the four-armed signpost and continue along the top of the downs. There is a wired enclosure to the left, often with goats grazing, and a seat on the right. After about $^1/_4$ mile we go through a strip of woodland to cross a stile into a large field, where we turn right then left, following the edge of the field and gradually going downhill. At the end we bear right through a few trees to a stile and a road.

2. Crossing the road and through a few trees we turn left on a drive for a short distance to a signposted footpath on the right. At first we have woods on both sides of the path and then a large open field on the left. At the end of the field on the left we turn left over a stile and go uphill with woods on the right. At the top with a stile to the right we turn left and continue along the top of the field then gradually drop down to a stile, on the right, which we cross. Going gently uphill we have Ruffett Wood on our right and at the end of this wood we go through the hedge and continue direction along a wide track at the edge of fields, finally over a stile opposite Perrotts Farm.

3. Bearing left across a wide farm track we enter Banstead Wood by a kissing gate and go forward to a wide track. At a seat on the left we turn right on a wide track with a waymark and in just under $^1/_4$ mile pass a small pond and seat on the left. We

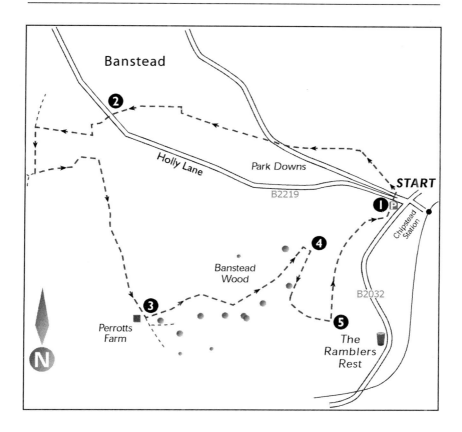

Banstead

❷

Holly Lane

Park Downs

START

B2219

❶ P

Chipstead Station

❹

Banstead
Wood

B2032

❸

❺

Perrotts
Farm

The
Ramblers
Rest

Ⓝ

continue on this wide track for some distance and take the third
wide turning on the right which doubles back slightly.

4. Soon reaching open hillside with good views and a seat
tucked into the hedge we turn right with the woods and another
seat soon on our right. Passing a belt of trees on the left we turn
left and take a diagonal path across the meadow to go through a
gap in the hedge and downhill, with another seat on the right.

For refreshment we can continue downhill bearing slightly
left to enter the car park of the Ramblers Rest. To return to the
walk, we retrace our steps uphill to turn right immediately after
the hedge.

Blackthorn can be seen in abundance

5. At a hedge (not the field edge) we turn left, keeping it close on our right, and follow a path for just over $^1/_2$ mile, sometimes in woods, sometimes on the open hillside. As we approach the car park the left fork takes us into the car park and the right fork will take us back to the grassy area to return to the station or the bus terminus.

Refreshments: The Ramblers Rest in Outwood Lane and also for bus passengers the Midday Sun in Chipstead Valley Road.

CHIPSTEAD: BANSTEAD WOOD AND CHIPHOUSE WOOD

Bluebells in Banstead Wood

This delightful walk, although close to built up areas, is entirely on footpaths and the few uphill sections lead to fine viewpoints. In spring the woods are full of wood anemones and bluebells and there are cowslips on the downs. In just a few miles we can enjoy a variety of countryside: woods, downland and farmland.

- **HOW TO GET THERE:** By train to Chipstead station, then go down Station Approach and turn left on the main road, crossing to a gate on the right. Go along a strip of grassland to arrive at the car park. By bus, alight at the Midday Sun in Chipstead Valley Road and walk along the road for just over $^1/_2$ mile to the car park.
- **PARKING:** Banstead Wood car park in Holly Lane.
- **LENGTH OF THE WALK:** 5 miles. Map: OS Explorer 146 (GR 277583).

THE WALK

1. With our backs to the road we leave the car park at the far right hand corner, entering a field. Keeping the woods on our left for some way we turn left into them at the first gate, by a seat, going steeply uphill, over a crossing path, to a wider track where we turn right. We ignore the first major left turn but at a junction of paths just after it, we turn left uphill and when this track flattens we take the second of two paths on the right. Following this twisting path for some distance we eventually go under a fallen tree and fork right to emerge on a wider path where we turn left. Turning left again, we see the buildings of Perrotts Farm ahead, and we turn left on a path, with a barrier and green notice board, following it to a wider track. Here we turn right, passing a stile on the left and bearing right to leave the woods by a kissing gate.

2. Bearing left across a farm track we go over a stile to a path with the hedge on our left which we follow for some distance. Reaching a wood we turn right then left to go down the edge of a field with the trees on our left. At the end of the wood we cross a stile and turn left along the edge of a field and in the top left hand corner cross another stile into trees. When the path forks we keep left to cross another stile and at the end of woods on the right go over another stile to take a diagonal path across a field to a hedgerow ahead. Here we turn left and follow the field boundary. A stile takes us past some cottages and out to a farm track where we turn left.

3. Just after passing a signpost on our right we keep ahead through a gate on the right and go down an enclosed path and eventually under a railway bridge. Turning left we enter Chiphouse Wood, managed by the Woodland Trust, and in about $1/2$ mile turn left under a railway bridge. A narrow path on the right takes us gradually uphill. Ignoring a left turn we go over a crossing path and continue up to a signpost. We take the path on the right signposted to Holly Lane car park and shortly fork left out into an open field where we keep the hedge on our right. At a crossing cart track we turn right,

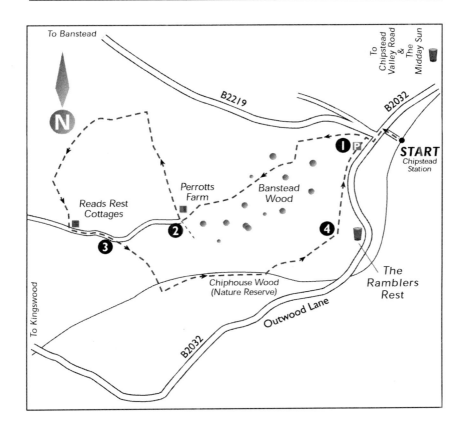

going gently downhill on this grassy track with a hedgerow on the left and open fields on the right. For refreshment, continue down to the road and the Ramblers Rest.

4. To continue the walk, at the end of the hedge on the left we turn left across the downs with trees over to the left and the road parallel down to the right. Maintaining direction we eventually go through a strip of trees where we turn left for the car park or right to the road which we cross for the station. For the bus we continue along the road to the bus terminus.

Refreshments: The Ramblers Rest in Outwood Lane and also for bus passengers the Midday Sun in Chipstead Valley Road.

KINGSWOOD

❦

View from the path near Reeves Rest

This country walk through farmland, crop fields and some woodland is a delight in all seasons. There are fine views to be enjoyed and just a few stiles.

- **HOW TO GET THERE:** By train to Kingswood station.
- **PARKING:** In the small car park at the station.
- **LENGTH OF THE WALK:** 6 miles. Map: OS Explorer 146 (GR 248566).

THE WALK

1. Leaving the station we turn right then right again along St Monica's Road. When this turns left we continue straight ahead on a small humped road which leads to a private car park which we cross to a footpath through open woodland. At a

Keepers Cottage

signpost, with a hedge ahead, we turn right downhill to cross the railway, following the path past some houses. At the road we cross to a signposted footpath opposite between houses. This footpath crosses two more roads and eventually we meet a road junction. Continuing direction we keep on the right hand pavement, following it round in front of houses, then continue ahead on an enclosed path, with a conifer hedge, which leads to a main road. We cross to a signposted footpath opposite, through a gate, and maintain direction over a golf course, later avoiding a driving range. At the end of the golf course we go through woods to a stile taking us into a sloping field. We continue downhill, with the hedge on our left, and at the bottom we cross another stile and the road with the Well House Inn on our left.

2. We go up a footpath by the side of the pub, then through a gate into an enclosed footpath alongside a field. Another gate takes us into an open field and, still keeping the hedge on our right, we continue to another gate leading into a narrow path. We soon reach a small road which we cross to another

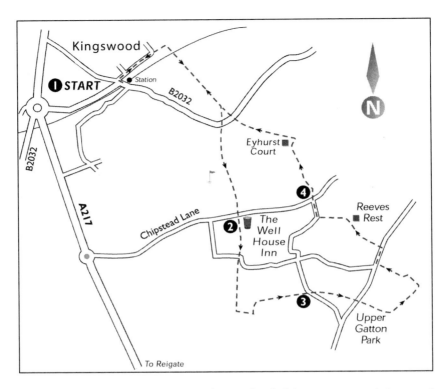

signposted enclosed footpath with fields on our right and gardens on the left. At another small road we cross to a signposted footpath opposite and soon cross a stile into a large field, keeping the hedge on our right. At a gate and hedge we turn left along the field boundary and at the corner left again to a signposted stile and gap in the hedge on the right. With a strip of woodland on our left we go uphill and continue along the edge of open fields with extensive views to the left, going through a gate and stile. A final gate takes us out to the road by the side of a cottage that usually has a colourful flower border alongside the footpath.

3. Crossing the road we take the signposted footpath opposite and cross a stile into a large open field, keeping the hedge on our left. After going down and partially up a small dip we turn right towards three freestanding trees and keeping

The handsome mansion of Upper Gatton Park can be seen from the route

them on our left we make for a stile in the hedge ahead. At the road we cross diagonally right to a narrow signposted footpath by the side of a house, crossing the stile at the end into an open field with a view of a large mansion, Upper Gatton Park, over to the right. With the woods on our left we continue through the field to the end then cross a stile into Upper Gatton Wood. There is an old World War II pillbox at the beginning and we follow a wide path, through the woods, ignoring side turnings. Leaving the wood, by a stile, into a sloping field we continue with the woods on our left to a crossing bridleway where we turn left through a gate and stile. Still with the woods close on our left, we go through another gate and stile and after the third gate we bear diagonally right across a small paddock. Crossing a stile we maintain direction on a farm road, with Park Farm buildings on the right, to reach a road where we turn right for about 100 yards. At the signposted footpath on the left we cross a stile into an enclosed path and, maintaining direction over stiles, we pass buildings on our right to continue forward into woodland.

The path narrows and twists downhill, in places quite steeply, but there is a handrail for the steepest part. A gate brings us out to a field and we follow a very well defined path downhill and then uphill to go through a gate to the road where we turn right downhill (we can avoid the road by taking the horse ride at the gate and turning right downhill parallel with the road, coming out at the bottom).

4. At the T-junction we cross to a signposted bridleway opposite and go gradually uphill with pleasant aspects and open fields all round until we reach Eyhurst Court on the left. At the small ornamental pond we turn left to follow the blue waymarked drive down to the road.

Again we cross to a signposted footpath opposite and at the end cross a road to continue on the pavement, soon reaching the footpath between houses we used at the beginning of the walk. We now retrace our steps back to Kingswood station by following the path over two more roads, then downhill to cross the railway. We continue uphill to the signpost, turn left through trees to St Monica's Road and finally left down to the station.

Refreshments: The Well House Inn at Mugswell.

TADWORTH AND WALTON HEATH

The marvellous view to be enjoyed from the top of Colley Hill

This is an exhilarating walk over the open spaces of Walton Heath with very gentle gradients and no stiles. The walk onto Colley Hill is well worth it for the marvellous views on offer.

- **HOW TO GET THERE:** By train or bus to Tadworth station.
- **PARKING:** In the station car park.
- **LENGTH OF THE WALK:** 5 miles; including Colley Hill $6^3/_4$ miles. Map: OS Explorer 146 (GR 231563).

THE WALK

1. Leaving Tadworth station from platform 2 we turn left into The Avenue and straight up to Station Approach, turning right along an enclosed footpath just before Barclay's Bank. On reaching a road we turn right for a few yards then left along a

45

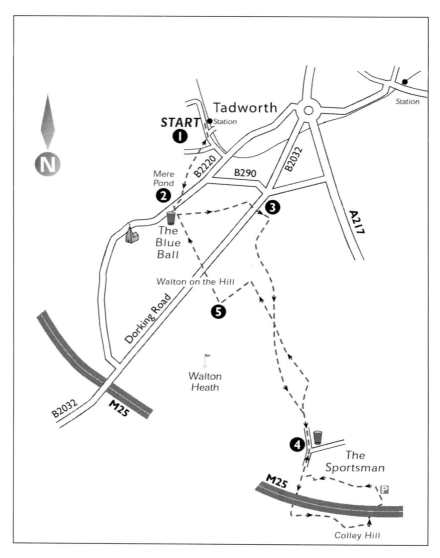

signposted bridleway onto heathland. There are several paths ahead of us and we take the tarmac path to the left signposted 'Mere Road'. At the road we turn right to Mere Pond where there are several seats and a variety of wildfowl.

If we wish to visit the church we walk along the main road, with the pond on our right, for a short distance. The church is generally unlocked and has an 800 year old lead font, considered to be one of the best of 38 lead fonts in England and the only one in Surrey.

2. To continue the walk from the pond we cross the road onto the corner of the heath (with the Blue Ball over on the right) and turn diagonally left on a gravel path, presently crossing a tarmac footpath. Soon, at a junction of paths, we take the one with four short vertical posts across it (second on the left) and follow it through a picnic area. Maintaining direction we cross a bridleway and pass a seat to a junction of 6 or 7 paths where we turn right on a well defined path towards a few pine trees. Keeping to the main path we reach a wider crossing path and cross to a small path opposite. This path bears left and soon, at a fork, we go right and right again at the next fork. At posts we cross a bridleway into a playing field and with woodland on our left we reach Dorking Road.

3. Crossing the road we go through a barrier onto Walton Heath and continue ahead towards a belt of trees where we turn right, gently downhill. Keeping the next belt of trees on our right we continue downhill to the bottom corner of the field. Crossing a bridleway we enter woods and continue over another bridleway on a small path. When this forks we take the right hand path and maintain direction across a pleasant area of open wooded heathland. Later, after going through a more open area, the path forks and either route will take us to a crossing bridleway where we turn right for a few yards to a junction of paths.

We pass waymarks in the hedge end and turn left on a path downhill with a hedge over to our left. At the bottom, after going through a hedge, we take the right fork and, ignoring all side turnings, follow this path for just over $1/2$ mile to reach the Sportsman.

For the longer walk to Colley Hill:
4. Passing the Sportsman on our left we reach a road junction where we bear right and follow the road, later going over the M25 motorway. At the end of the road, by some houses, we turn

The path across Walton Heath

left on the North Downs Way, a wide track through trees. On reaching a gate we bear right out onto Colley Hill. Turning left along the top of the hill we can enjoy extensive views. Later, keeping close to the hedge on our left, we turn left, cross a gravel path and go through a gate with a water tower on our right. Following this narrow path we cross the motorway, and continue through woods to a small National Trust car park. Leaving the car park we turn left and left again, with the car park now on our left and open fields on our right. Later we cross a small road and continue on a bridleway to another road where we turn right. At the road junction we turn left back to the Sportsman.

Both routes now continue together: With the Sportsman on our right we go onto the open heath, keeping trees on our right. In about ¹/₂ mile there is a four-armed signpost on the left, rather hidden by a group of trees. Here we turn left on a narrow path through a patch of scrub emerging onto open heathland. We follow this little path for some distance, ignoring all side turnings, finally bearing left at a junction. Later we go downhill, passing some trees, and continue ahead uphill to trees at the top. Here we turn left and keeping the trees on our right reach a golf course.

5. At the golf course we turn right and, keeping it on our left, continue on this path for about $^1/_2$ mile. Soon after passing a waymarked bridleway on the right, the track forks and we take the right hand fork, eventually reaching Dorking Road which we cross to a sign 'Walton House'. On the right is a footpath, soon signposted to 'Mere Pond', which we follow, at first gently uphill. On reaching the road we cross to the pond and turn right, soon to turn left on the path we were on earlier. At a road, we turn right and then left on the enclosed footpath back to the station.

Refreshments: The Sportsman at Mogador and the Blue Ball near Mere Pond.

ASHTEAD COMMON

Ashtead Common

This walk is especially attractive in spring or late autumn when there are no leaves on the trees to obscure the view and the rich brown of the bracken makes a superb backdrop. The walk takes us through an interesting area where the skeletal remains of once noble trees still stand after devastating fires in 1984 and 1990. Deer are frequently seen in the woodland glades. Once we have left the railway station, we encounter no roads or stiles.

- **HOW TO GET THERE:** By train to Ashtead station or by bus to Ashtead and then $^1/_2$ mile down the road to the station.
- **PARKING:** At the railway station.
- **LENGTH OF THE WALK:** 5 miles. Maps: OS Explorer 146 and 161 (GR 180590).

THE WALK

1. We leave the station and take the gravel path opposite the level crossing barrier onto the common, finally crossing a bridge and turning left. This path leads to a crossing track with a bridge and some houses to the left but we turn right through a brushwood fence, going gently uphill. At a crossing track we turn left and follow this path to a junction of paths where there is an information board to the left. We continue ahead for some distance. At a waymarked post on the left we turn right on a small path through trees, slightly doubling back.

Maintaining direction we pass a waymark post on the right, then another, and continue to a junction of wide grassy tracks. Turning left we go gently uphill, ignoring all crossing paths. At the top, there is a seat to the right, but we keep to the left and soon fork right. After a short distance, we continue through a barrier and across a grit track to a small path opposite.

2. If refreshments are required we can turn left down the grit track and along a drive out to the road where, turning right for a few yards, there is the Star. We retrace our steps turning left on the drive, passing the stable on our left, and turning right at the information board. Passing a waymark and a barrier on the right and going gently uphill we take the first path on the left.

This path becomes a wide grassy track which we follow, ignoring a left fork, eventually reaching a wide open grassy area and junction of paths. We continue direction gently uphill and after a barrier we turn left downhill. Reaching a wide bridleway we turn right with fields on our left, later passing information boards at a signpost on the right.

(The walk can be shortened here by turning right and continuing across the common to Ashtead station.)

3. To continue the walk we follow the track with fields on the left for just under $^1/_2$ mile ignoring all side turnings and dropping down to a small lake used by fishermen. Keeping the lake close on our right we walk round it until at the end, immediately after four concrete paving blocks in the path, we turn left and go up steps to a larger lake where we turn right.

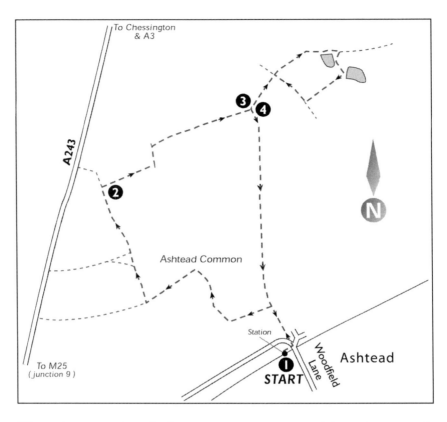

There is a seat just before we enter trees and ignoring a path over a plank bridge on our left we follow a twisting path. Taking the first left turning, we eventually come out to a wider bridleway. Turning right we soon reach the wide track we were on earlier and turn left, now with fields on our right, back to the information boards and signpost.

4. Turning left we soon fork right and following the blue bridleway waymarks we pass a small pond with a seat where we may watch the dragonflies and, if we are lucky, a deer coming down to drink. The track continues gently downhill to the bridge and gravel track back to Ashtead station.

Refreshments: The Star at Malden Rushett on the A243.

LEATHERHEAD

The magnificent view from Norbury Park

BOCKETTS FARM, NORBURY PARK AND THE RIVER MOLE

This is a varied walk through woods, over downland and along the river with some good views and an opportunity to visit Bocketts Farm where there are some rare breeds of domestic animals. It is suitable for any time of the year and there are no stiles.

- **HOW TO GET THERE:** By train or bus to Leatherhead.
- **PARKING:** At the Leisure Centre, just off the B2122, in Leatherhead.
- **LENGTH OF THE WALK:** $5^1/_2$ miles. Map: OS Explorer 146 (GR 163568).

THE WALK

1. From the railway station we turn down the approach road and cross a road by traffic lights to continue direction with the

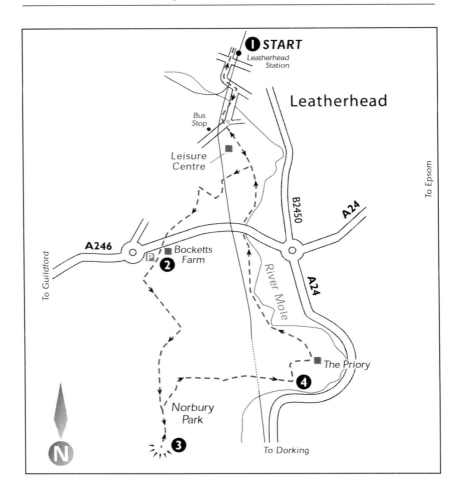

railway on our right, crossing another small road. At the main road we cross by the traffic lights under the bridge with the bus station on the right, and continue forward to the Leisure Centre.

Keeping the Centre on our right we come to a barrier and turn right up a bridleway, soon going over a railway bridge. Keeping to the main path we pass a small metal fenced enclosure where we bear right to a field and turn right, gradually going uphill. At the top, by a signpost we turn left and follow

Rare breeds at Bocketts Farm

this bridleway to a road; there are good views to the left and in spring the fields on the right are carpeted with cowslips. We cross the road with care to a signposted bridleway opposite with Bocketts Farm on the left.

Bocketts Farm, which is open throughout the year apart from at Christmas, is now a visitor centre for rare breeds of domestic animals and includes a café and shop.

2. We follow the bridleway and at the end of farm fields on our left turn left up a signposted bridleway, going gently uphill. At the top by a signpost we turn right for a short distance and at a bend turn right through a barrier with a rather hidden signpost on the right. This path takes us along the top of the downs with many chalkland wildflowers and pleasant aspects, eventually going through a barrier. Bearing left we join a wide vehicle track and bear left with the sawmills of Norbury Park on our right and soon passing a picnic area on our left.

At the main drive we turn right through another barrier and at the end of wire fencing on the left turn left, following the fence. On reaching the corner of the fence we bear right to the viewpoint and a seat with magnificent views towards Box Hill and Juniper Top.

3. After resting for a while we retrace our steps back to the main drive and turn right, soon passing the sawmills again. We pass the main entrance gates to Norbury Park House and take a signposted bridleway on the right – there is a seat at the start. The track crosses a drive to another entrance into Norbury Park House and we go through posts to follow the bridleway, eventually going through a barrier and joining a tarmac drive.

4. Going down the drive we finally turn left at a junction to pass The Priory, soon bearing left through a waymarked gate. We now follow this track, with the River Mole nearby on our right, for over a mile going through various gates, passing a picnic area, continuing under a bridge and eventually reaching the gate to the Leisure Centre which we pass on our left.

We now retrace our steps back to the bus station or railway station.

Refreshments: Bocketts Farm or one of the many inns and cafés in Leatherhead.

BOOKHAM COMMON

A rustic plank bridge on Bookham Common

This walk takes us through the woods and common land of Bookham Common to farm fields with grazing llamas. Deer are likely to be seen and there are wildfowl on the several ponds. Bookham Common is a wet common, though, and best avoided after spells of heavy rain.

- **HOW TO GET THERE:** By train to Bookham station.
- **PARKING:** At the railway station.
- **LENGTH OF THE WALK:** $5^1/_2$ miles. Map: OS Explorer 146 (GR 127556).

THE WALK

1. From the station we go through the car park to the road and turn left. When the road turns right, we go left through a small

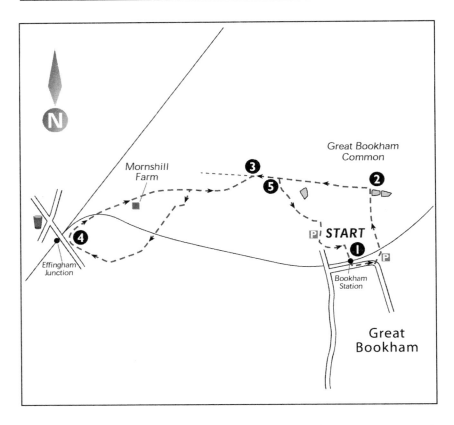

National Trust car park on the main track. We pass a vehicle track on the left and within a few yards turn left on a small path into trees. At a fork we keep right and go over several crossing paths through this pleasant open woodland. Later the path bears right and after passing a pond on our right, we reach a bridleway.

2. At the main bridleway we turn left, passing two more small ponds with many ducks. We go through a barrier on the left, turn left on a smaller path and then left over planking across marshy ground to reach the largest pond on Bookham Common. There are several seats where we may rest and watch the wildlife; often a heron can be seen near the small island in the pond. Keeping the pond on our right we go through posts into a wider track where we turn right. The track turns right and we pass an

Negotiating a stile

information board on our left. At a crossing track we turn left very soon, taking the track signposted to Effingham Common.

3. We follow the hedged track for some distance before we pass a complex of houses. The track becomes narrower and we have a field on our right and after about $^{1}/_{4}$ mile, at the end of the field, there is a National Trust sign and we ignore a footpath turning off to the right. In a few yards we turn left on a small waymarked path into trees.

A stile takes us into a wide enclosed path with a hedge on the right and open fields on our left. At a gate on the right there are some information boards about the llamas that may be grazing in these fields. Two more stiles take us under the railway into an open field with a stream on our left. At the end of the field is another stile taking us into a wide track with a house and garden on the left. A final stile goes into a wide grassy track which we cross to enter woods opposite and emerge at a tarmac drive where we turn right.

4. For refreshment we turn left at the tarmac drive, continue along to the road and turning right go over the railway to a junction and the *Lord Howard*. Retracing our steps we go back over the railway and turn left along the tarmac drive.

After going under the railway bridge the drive turns right into a farm while we continue straight ahead on a signposted bridleway. Later we pass Mornsill Farm on the right and continue on the track, ignoring side turnings, passing the turning we took earlier. We retrace part of the walk we did earlier and when we reach a signpost we take the path signposted to Great Bookham and very soon turn right on a narrow path to a gate visible in the trees.

5. We go forward over the open common on a grass track with low scrub on either side. Later we maintain direction over a junction of paths and presently bear slightly right to cross a plank bridge. We shortly ignore two left forks and keeping on the main path eventually reach a gate into a small car park which we cross to another gate. Maintaining our direction we later go through a gate and soon turn sharply right on a narrow path which brings us out to the upside platform of Bookham station.

Refreshments: The Lord Howard pub at Effingham Junction.

EFFINGHAM COMMON AND LITTLE BOOKHAM

❧❀❧

Little Bookham church

This is a pleasant walk on level ground through woods and farmland and includes some very attractive manmade lakes with a variety of wildfowl. We pass Little Bookham church, which has been there for 900 years, alongside an equally ancient yew tree.

- **HOW TO GET THERE:** By train to Effingham Junction station.
- **PARKING:** At the railway station.
- **LENGTH OF THE WALK:** 5¹/₂ miles. Map: OS Explorer 146 (GR 103559).

THE WALK

1. Leaving the downside platform of Effingham Junction station we turn right down the road and right again on a signposted

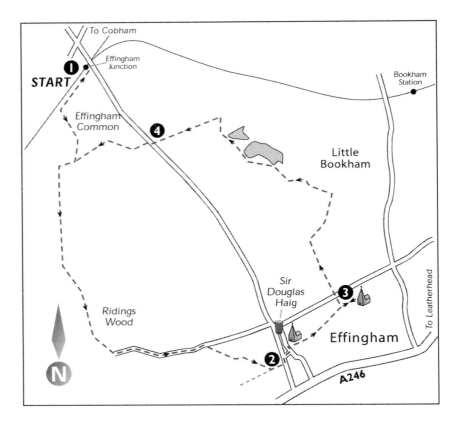

bridleway, passing the car park. After going through posts, with the common on our left and some bungalows on the right, we turn left onto the common and bear right, with woods on our right. Later on the path becomes more distinct and on reaching a hedge we continue, keeping the hedge and gardens on our right. At the end of this long field we cross a drive to a signposted bridleway (not the signposted footpath next to it) and continue on the bridleway for about ¹/₂ mile with Ridings Wood, managed by the Woodland Trust, on the left. A signposted track goes off to the right but we keep straight on, now with a brick wall on the right. At brick gateposts on the right we turn left on a wide track going gently downhill which later becomes a residential lane. The lane goes slightly uphill and at the top, opposite a house called Hartfield, we turn right on an enclosed path next to a drive. When this ends we continue diagonally across a field to a stile where we turn left, soon coming to Effingham village.

Refreshments are available at the Sir Douglas Haig if we turn left down through the village and there are shops if we turn right.

2. To continue, we cross the road slightly left to a road called Crossways at the end of which we bear left into the churchyard of St Lawrence's church. Passing the church on our left we bear right on a footpath, enclosed at first, which we follow for about $^1/_4$ mile, passing a school, to reach Little Bookham church. Much of the church is 900 years old and on the south side, from the outside, we can still see where the pillars and arches were when a former aisle was demolished and filled in. The nearby yew tree is just as old.

3. After visiting the church we retrace our steps back along the way we came and very soon turn right on a footpath, with the school on our left. At the road we cross slightly right to a footpath at the end of which we bear left, taking us through a strip of open woodland. Reaching a wide track we bear left and follow this, with woods on our right and open fields on our left. At a gate across the track we turn left through a squeeze stile, going along the fence and through two more squeeze stiles. We now go diagonally across the next field to another stile and lakes ahead. We follow the waymarks through several more squeeze stiles, the first of which is soon on our left. Bearing right round the lakes we reach a squeeze stile in the field corner, cross a plank bridge and turn left then immediately right across a gravel drive. A broad bridge takes us over another lake and after another stile we go up a slope and along the edge of a field, with trees on our left. Shortly we turn left over a ladder stile and go down a pleasant residential road to the main road which we cross to a signposted footpath opposite.

4. Going forward we continue through a wicket gate, keeping along the hedge on the right. This public footpath goes through

The route takes us through the churchyard at St Lawrence's church, Effingham

a private garden so please respect the owners' privacy. Coming out on a drive we reach a cricket ground and maintaining direction we pass in front of the cricket pavilion and keep along the edge of the field to cross a stile in the corner. Turning left we follow the rough path across the common to trees ahead. Here we turn right and retrace the way we came earlier, back to the bridleway, through the posts and past the car park to turn left up the road to the station.

Refreshments: The Sir Douglas Haig pub in Effingham village.

GOMSHALL, ABINGER AND BROOMY DOWNS

Gomshall

This varied walk is pleasant all year round. In spring the snowdrops are a delight and in summer there are poppies and corn marigolds in the fields near Abinger Common. Stout footwear is recommended for wetter days.

- **HOW TO GET THERE:** By train or bus to Gomshall station.
- **PARKING:** At the railway station.
- **LENGTH OF THE WALK:** $5^1/_4$ miles. Maps: OS Explorers 145 and 146 (GR 089479).

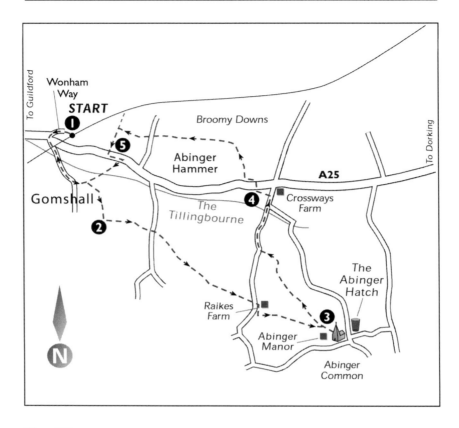

THE WALK

1. Leaving Gomshall station approach we cross the main road to turn left under the railway by the pedestrian tunnel and turn right along Wonham Way. We follow the lane as it turns left but when it later bends right we turn left at the side of the first house, then bear diagonally right across a field behind houses. A stile in the hedgerow takes us into a sunken bridleway in which we turn right, shortly going over another stile on our left.

2. Keeping the hedge on our right we go along the edge of the field and at a signpost we turn left across the middle of a field with a few isolated trees on our left. At the end of the field we go over a stile and turn right on a narrow enclosed path and then, bearing left, go down to a road.

We cross to a stile opposite, go over a stream and along the fence with a Woodland Trust wood on our right. At the end of the wood we enter a field and follow the line of telegraph poles on a well-defined path. Just after a track feeds in from the left, and as the path turns right, we go through a gap in the hedge ahead and across fields diagonally, making for Raikes Farm which can be seen ahead, and the road.

Crossing the road diagonally right we take a signposted footpath through farm buildings, immediately bearing right on a gravel drive to a track which soon bears left. We follow this track for nearly ¹/₂ mile and after taking us over open fields it becomes enclosed as it borders the grounds of Abinger Manor. At the gateway of the manor we take a small path leading into the churchyard of Abinger church with the Abinger Hatch opposite.

The church, which dates from the 11th century, was extensively restored in 1951 after being partly destroyed by enemy action in 1944. There are some ancient stocks on the green outside the church and some seats.

3. To continue the walk we retrace our steps through the churchyard to the beginning of the track round Abinger Manor and immediately after the cattle grid we turn right on a waymarked path, following the hedge on our left. We continue down this pleasant valley with good views ahead. In about ¹/₂ mile, at the end of the hedge, the path turns right and then soon left still with a hedge on our left. Immediately, at an opening on the left leading back down to the road, we take a small path in the hedge, often obscured by growth in summer.

The path takes us down to the road where we turn right, later passing some cottages on our left and a small road on our right. Immediately after crossing a stream we go over a stile on our left and diagonally across a meadow towards a house on the far side of the road, with 17th century Crossways Farm on our right.

4. On reaching the road we cross to a footpath opposite. This path is a delight at all seasons, snowdrops in spring and many

The village stocks at Abinger

other unusual wild flowers planted by the owner. As the footpath ends we enter a field by a stile and continue forward with some isolated trees on our right, making for a stile into woods. We go forward and over a crossing track, soon bearing left through an open area, to reach the open green of Broomy Downs. There is a seat over to the right under some trees.

From the open green we maintain our original direction, taking the main path which later goes slightly downhill to a gate through which we continue forward on a field path, keeping the hedge on our left. Another gate takes us to a road which we cross to a signposted footpath opposite, passing a house on our left and entering a wood by a stile. We maintain direction through the wood and come out to a lane where we turn left down to the main road.

5. We cross the road, turning left, and in about 100 yards turn right on a signposted bridleway. Crossing over a bridge spanning the Tillingbourne, we shortly take a path to the left of a drive, at first through trees, then along the edge of a field. We come out

The Abinger Hatch inn makes a good stopping place for a relaxing drink

to a lane in which we turn right and follow it back to the main road and railway bridge at Gomshall station.

Refreshments: At the Abinger Hatch in Abinger Common, and at Gomshall.

GOMSHALL, ALBURY HEATH AND SHERE

❧❧❧

St James's church nestles in the village of Shere

A walk which crosses over heathland, farmland and woodland, and is suitable for any time of the year but particularly recommended for late February when snowdrops will be seen and also new lambs in the fields around Shere. It also gives us the opportunity to visit the ancient church at Albury.

- **HOW TO GET THERE:** By train or bus to Gomshall station.
- **PARKING:** At the railway station.
- **LENGTH OF THE WALK:** 6 miles. Map: OS Explorer 145 (GR 089479).

THE WALK

1. Leaving Gomshall station approach we cross the main road to turn left under the railway by the pedestrian tunnel and turn

70

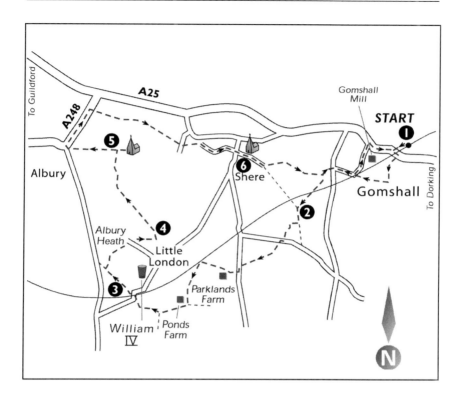

right along Wonham Way, a stony track. As the track turns sharply left we turn right along an enclosed footpath with a large house over on the right and farm buildings on the left. At the end of the path we turn right under the railway bridge and then left along a small road to a junction. We go straight across to a bridleway, soon bearing left. The track forks and we keep left passing a house and after going over a railway we bear left shortly to join a path coming from the right.

2. At a brick wall on the right we turn right into the trees and follow this path which turns sharply left bringing us out to a road. We turn right for a few yards then turn left on a signposted footpath, keeping the fence on our right and with wide views on our left. We continue across a meadow and within the wood on

71

our right we may get a glimpse of snowdrops in season. At a road we cross to a path immediately opposite, eventually coming out on a tarmac drive where we turn right. Passing white painted level crossing gates we turn left, soon on a sunken bridleway, to Ponds Farm on the right. We turn right by a yard, crossing two stiles, to join a drive and eventually reach a road where we turn right to go under a railway bridge.

If we want refreshment the William IV inn is a short distance up the road in Little London.

3. To continue the walk, immediately under the railway bridge we turn left up a signposted footpath onto Albury Heath, passing a small brick building on the right. We cross a wider track and take the right hand of two small paths. There are many seats on Albury Heath, and it is an ideal spot for a picnic. At a junction of paths we take the second on the right, a wider path, bearing round to the right and continue with houses down on our right. Following this wide, open path we reach a rough drive where we turn left and shortly reach a road where we turn right.

4. At a bend in the road there are three signposted footpaths on the left and we take the left hand one, going through a metal gate in front of South Lodge Cottage. This is the public footpath to Albury church through the private estate of Albury Park. Soon after entering the park, and just before a gate ahead, we turn left by a waymarked post. The path is well waymarked throughout and eventually drops down to turn right, through a gate and over a drive to a little church on the right. There are many snowdrops around the church and in the park on the other side of the wall in early spring.

The church was once the centre of a thriving village and dates back to Saxon times. The doorway dates from 1240 and the porch was added in the 15th century. There is a great deal to interest the visitor, in particular a very dramatic medieval wall-painting and a highly decorated 19th century chapel designed by Augustus Pugin. The many booklets and leaflets available in the church will give a better background and make the visit more enjoyable. The Mansion in Albury Park goes back

A Victorian letterbox still in use on the edge of the footpath

to 1042 but has been rebuilt many times. It is currently open to the public from May to September, 2 pm to 5 pm, Wednesdays and Thursdays.

5. With the church behind us we walk down the drive, which is not a public right of way but a permissive path for visiting the church, passing the lodge house and turning right into the road, soon right again into the main road. Just after passing a large church on the right we turn right up a signposted track with a Victorian letterbox at the corner. A stile takes us into a pleasant meadow, going gently uphill with good views to reach another stile taking us through woods. Leaving the woods by a gate we cross another meadow to a further strip of wood and drop down to a small lane where we turn right. After crossing a ford we turn left through a gate (look out for grey wagtails foraging in the shallows) following the river to another gate leading to a small road on the outskirts of Shere. Passing some delightful houses on the right we come to the main street of Shere by a bridge. (There are toilets just to the left.)

6. We cross the main street to a small road leading to the unlocked church which is well worth a visit. It goes back 600 years and some parts may be Saxon. At the end of the houses on the right we go through a gate to an enclosed footpath (new lambs are often in the fields round here in early spring). At the end of this enclosed path, we turn left with the hedge on our left and continue to a lane where we turn left out to a road junction.

We take the road straight ahead, turning left at the railway bridge we came under earlier, and out to the main road at Gomshall Mill. Turning right on the main road we pass a restaurant on the left and Gomshall station is just beyond.

Refreshments: Inns at Gomshall, Shere and the William IV at Little London.

SHALFORD AND THE CHANTRIES

The River Wey at Shalford

This is a varied walk across farmland, over downland giving extensive views, through Chantries woods and alongside the Wey Navigation Canal with boats plying back and forth. There are a couple of uphill gradients and just two stiles but all well worth the effort.

- **HOW TO GET THERE:** By train or bus to Shalford station.
- **PARKING:** At the railway station.
- **LENGTH OF THE WALK:** $5^1/_2$ miles. Map: OS Explorer 145 (GR 003471).

THE WALK

1. Leaving Shalford station on the south side we go up to a road and turn left, passing some shops, the Methodist church and a few houses. The path bears away from the road to go in front of some attractive cottages and onto the green. We cross a small road, continuing ahead on a tarmac path along which are several seats and a children's playground on the left. We reach a gravel drive with a house on the left and turn left on a small road. The road bears left at a brick wall and we turn right into an enclosed path with a fence on the left and open playing fields on the right. On reaching the railway line we turn right alongside it, soon passing a level crossing.

Following this enclosed path for almost $1/2$ mile we go through a gate and after a few yards, at a waymarked post, we turn left up steps to cross the railway. Going down steps the other side we go forward through another gate and through a strip of woods. On reaching a field we keep the hedge on our right, soon dropping down to pass a cottage on the left. We bear right on a track through trees, soon with buildings on the right, coming out eventually to a road where we turn left for a short distance.

2. At Halfpenny Corner we turn left and almost immediately right on a signposted uphill footpath. At a road we turn left for a few yards to a gate on the left into a crop field, following the hedge on our left. After passing a barn on our right the path goes gently uphill on a sandy track (notice the badger holes in the bank). After going downhill we turn right over a signposted stile and go diagonally right up a sloping field towards the end of a row of trees. Another stile takes us into open woodland and goes quite steeply uphill for a short distance. Looking to the right, when we reach the open, we can see St Martha's church.

3. At a crossing track we turn left on a wide grassy path along open hillside, with many downland flowers, giving extensive views. At the bend there is a seat where we can enjoy the view. The path bears right and soon left, keeping trees on our right. Just before the path goes downhill and by a seat, we turn right into the woodland of the Chantries. We soon turn left and left again and at a wide crossing track we turn left. There are many seats along the paths in these woods, an ideal spot for bird watching. At a small open space on the right there is an elegant

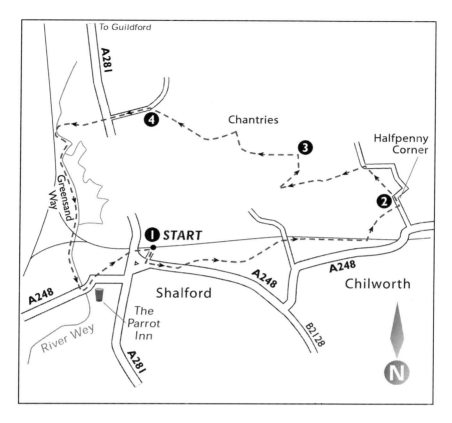

curved seat from where an unexpected 'keyhole' view of Guildford Cathedral can be seen. Returning to the track we turn right to resume our original direction, soon coming to a junction of paths. We turn left, going gradually downhill, eventually reaching the entrance to the Chantries with some excellent information boards.

4. Leaving the Chantries we turn right then left, passing a small car park on the right. The drive joins a pleasant residential road which we cross to turn left on the raised footpath. Reaching the main road we cross, on the crossing, and go straight across playing fields to an opening in the hedge ahead. The path goes over a stream and continues through a gate and across a meadow to reach the River Wey.

On the canal path near the Parrot Inn

Here we turn left to cross the river by the bridge, then walk southwards, following the river on our left. The river bears away to the left and we are now on the towpath of the Wey Navigation Canal. In summer months pleasure boats come from Guildford as far as the lock. We continue along the towpath for about a mile and when we reach the road turn left with the Parrot Inn on the right. Just round the bend of the road we take a signposted footpath on the left across a common. There are several signposted footpaths here but we take the one for cyclists and walkers. Reaching a few cottages we continue on a tarmac road, still following our signpost. At a car park on the left we cross it to the far corner to reach the main road. Crossing by the pedestrian lights we turn right and go down a few steps to the station approach and turn left for the station.

Refreshments: The Parrot Inn at Shalford.

GODALMING AND PEPER HAROW

❦

National Trust cottages alongside the River Wey at Lower Eashing

After walking alongside the River Wey, we continue into Peper Harow Park and on to the picturesque villages of Peper Harow and Eashing. We then cross the finest old bridge in Surrey, which is a popular subject for artists.

- **HOW TO GET THERE:** By train to Godalming station.
- **PARKING:** At the railway station.
- **LENGTH OF THE WALK:** $5^3/_4$ miles. Map: OS Explorer 145 (GR 966439).

THE WALK

1. We leave the station and bear left down the station approach soon to take a signposted pedestrian path on the left. Turning left down the road alongside the church we shortly take a signposted

79

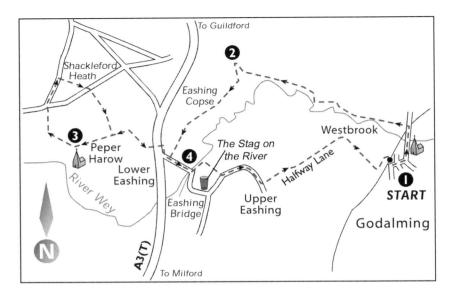

footpath on the left across the river and through a car park to rejoin the road before going under the railway. We turn left on a signposted path which takes us to the river which we follow to go over a footbridge and at a fork we bear left, leaving the tarmac path, to continue along the riverside. After about 400 yards we fork right and fork right again, passing a pillbox, to go alongside a garden and house to a road where we turn left to enter woodland.

2. After about ¹/₂ mile we join a tarmac track and soon turn left on a signposted bridleway which later joins a concrete drive and after some ³/₄ mile reaches the road, where we turn right. Shortly turning right again we join a path to cross the footbridge over the A3 and soon go through a gate. Turning right we follow the path round a field, going through a horse gate in the corner. Turning immediately left we cross a strip of woodland and maintaining direction we follow the path to the church and village of Peper Harow. The church has a Norman doorway and a Norman chancel arch but is only open for services.

3. After visiting the church we continue through the tiny village and along the drive to the road where we turn right and immediately left. After about 200 yards we turn right through Shackleford Heath on the main path until we reach a road which we cross. Maintaining direction we reach the horse gate which we negotiated earlier and follow the path round to the left finally to reach the footbridge over the A3.

We retrace our steps but pass the turning that we came from earlier and continue forward to go over Eashing Bridge, which was probably built by the monks from Waverley Abbey, and is now owned and cared for by the National Trust. There is an inn – the Stag on the River – further along the road in the village.

4. Immediately over the bridge we turn left on a signposted footpath alongside the river, later with a field on our left, and after a stile we cross a field finally to reach the road, where we turn left. After a sharp right hand bend in the road we turn left along a wide surfaced track and, after passing Halfway House, continue on the track round a sharp right bend, soon to take a path alongside a house. We continue down this path and join a metalled road that passes the entrance to the up platform at

The famous Eashing Bridge

The Stag on the River, at Lower Eashing

Godalming station. For the car park we continue and turn right under the railway to go through the lower car park and up steps to the higher car park and the station buildings.

Refreshments: At Godalming, and the Stag on the River at Lower Eashing.

THE RIVER WEY AND COMPTON

A tranquil spot on the Wey

This walk takes us beside the River Wey and along part of the North Downs Way through farm fields with wide-open views, to the tiny village of Compton. Along the way we pass the Watts Gallery, Compton's Norman church and Loseley House.

- **HOW TO GET THERE:** By train to Guildford station or Shalford station.
- **PARKING:** There is parking available at both railway stations.
- **LENGTH OF THE WALK:** $7^1/_2$ miles starting from Shalford station (GR 003471); 8 miles starting from Guildford station (GR 992496). Map: OS Explorer 145.

THE WALK

1A. Starting from Guildford station: We go forward towards a major road junction which we cross, using the subway, turning right up the ramp. Keeping Wey House, a red brick building, on our left, we drop down to the riverbank and turn right under the road bridge. With the river on our left we turn left in front of the White House onto a small path and we follow the river to cross it by the bridge on our left. We take the first turning on the right alongside Millmead Lock and cross a green, with many picnic tables on our left, to join the towpath where we turn right. After about 600 yards, and just before a bridge, we turn right alongside a house and up a tarmac drive.

1B. Starting from Shalford station: We leave the station on the southbound side and bear right up the approach road, soon turning right to cross the grass and go up steps to the road. Crossing by the pedestrian lights we go down past the local bottle bank to turn right on a minor road. Taking the left fork we soon pass houses and take the right hand path across the green to a road. We turn right and immediately after crossing Broadford Bridge, turn right again to join the River Wey towpath for nearly a mile, passing a lock. Later, after going under a bridge, we turn left at a North Downs waymark, to go alongside a house and up a tarmac drive.

2. Both versions now continue together: At the road we turn right and taking great care cross to go along the first road on the left, Sandy Lane. After about 200 yards we turn right onto a wide signposted bridleway (the North Downs Way) for some 2 miles, enjoying fine views of the downs. After passing Piccard's farmhouse we turn sharply left and then take the second path, a signposted bridleway, on the right. We maintain direction over crossing paths and after a mile or so finally reach the road at the Watts Gallery (open every afternoon except Thursday), where we turn left. Shortly we pass the cemetery and Watts Chapel, which is also well worth a visit. At the T-junction we turn left through the village of Compton, passing the church and the Harrow Inn, both on the right.

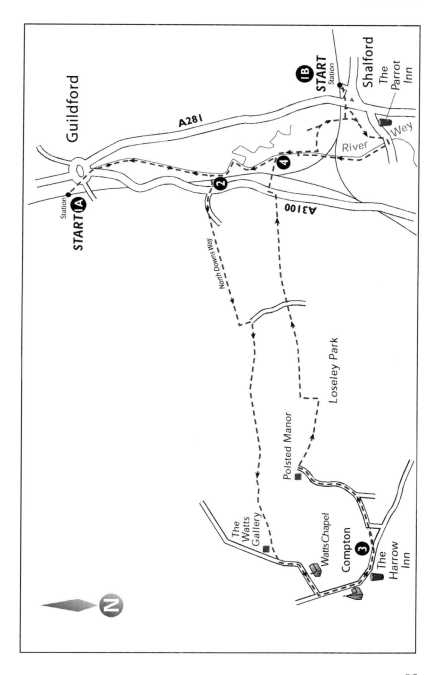

Watts Chapel at Compton

Detail on Watts Chapel

St Nicholas' church is more than 1,000 years old. The tower and some walls are Saxon but most of the church fabric is Norman, including the roof timbers, font, chancel screen and the scratched sketch of a knight on the wall by the pulpit. There is also a gallery above the altar.

3. At the end of the houses on the left we bear slightly left across a green to the right hand end of a row of houses. Going through a gap in the fence we turn left up the road which, keeping left at a junction, takes us to Polsted Manor. Here we turn right along a footpath and, at a gate signed 'Private', we turn sharply left over a stile, down the field. After another stile we follow the fence down and round to the right then to go over a double stile. With fine views of Loseley House on our right we go over a stile to skirt a pretty lake to another stile. Maintaining direction we pass two stately oak trees, cross a stile then another which takes us between houses. We reach a road and cross to a lane opposite which, after $^3/_4$ mile, brings us to a major road. Carefully crossing this, we turn left for a short distance to turn right on a signposted footpath. Going through an access barrier we continue under a railway bridge and reach the river at St Catherine's Lock.

4. For return to Guildford: At the bridge over the lock we turn left and follow the towpath for about a mile back through the picnic area. Later we go under a bridge and left past Wey House to the subway for the station.

For return to Shalford: We cross the bridge over the lock and turn right along the canal bank and, after a cottage, we go over a weir and turn left. Soon we turn right to join a wooden boardwalk taking us uphill, eventually through a gate to turn right on a track. Crossing a railway bridge we turn left and keep parallel with the railway line up through a small car park to the main road which we cross to the station approach.

Refreshments: The Tea Shop alongside the Watts Gallery, and the Harrow Inn at Compton.

WORMLEY AND HYDON'S BALL

A magical spot on the route

This walk is a mixture of open woodland, some farmland and lowland streams. In late spring bluebells are in abundance and in May there are rhododendrons. A short steep path leads up to the top of Hydon's Ball, where the view can be enjoyed from a welcome seat.

- **HOW TO GET THERE:** By train to Witley station.
- **PARKING:** At the railway station.
- **LENGTH OF THE WALK:** 6 miles. Map: OS Explorer 133 (GR 948380).

THE WALK

1. Crossing the footbridge to the up platform we take a signposted footpath at the down end of the platform. This path

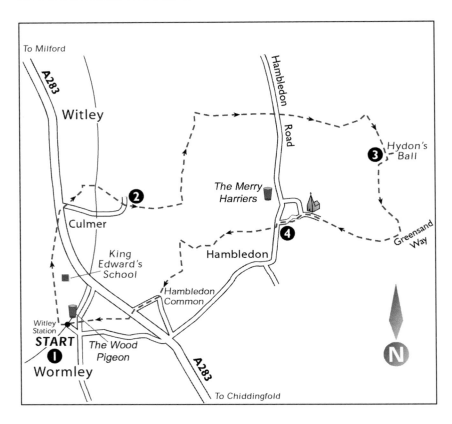

widens and takes us over a crossing track, across a road to an enclosed path and to a junction which we cross to a signposted footpath at the left hand side of a games field. Later we cross a main road to take a signposted footpath between hedges, on the left in Culmer Lane. Turning left at a T-junction we soon take a small path on the right, crossing a river, going under the railway and finally reaching a road which we cross to the signposted footpath (not bridleway) opposite.

2. With a golf course on our left we later enter woods and after a stile turn left, soon out in the open and, having passed a lake, take the right hand fork. In the right hand corner of the field we go through a barrier and alongside a drive to turn right over a footbridge into woodland. This pretty woodland path finally

A leafy glade in springtime

comes out at a golf course and keeping to the hedge on the left we go downhill to turn right on a crossing gravel track. We continue for about $^1/_2$ mile and at the road we cross to a signposted bridleway. After about 750 yards we turn right on a waymarked crossing path and go gently uphill.

3. At the top of the hill we can take a small path on the left which will take us up to the viewpoint on Hydon's Ball where there is a seat. With our backs to the seat we take the path to our right and forking right retrace our steps back to our original path where we turn left downhill and just after a memorial on the right we take a small path on the right. Continuing over a crossing track we take the next turning on the right, the Greensand Way, and enjoying fine views we finally reach a road by Hambledon church. Just along the road we take the right hand of two footpaths on the left soon to rejoin the road again and reach a T-junction.

Refreshments can be taken at the Merry Harriers about 200 yards along the road to the right but, unfortunately on this very narrow road, there is no footway.

4. Turning left for a short distance we turn right on a signposted footpath and eventually, after about $^1/_2$ mile, reach a cottage and a junction of paths where we turn sharp left. At the end of this path we come out on Hambledon Common and on our left there is a picturesque house. With our backs to this house we follow the wide sandy track ahead out to a road where we turn right along to a main road junction.

Crossing the road we turn left, soon to turn right on a signposted footpath between gardens which brings us out to the road opposite the station and car park.

Refreshments: The Merry Harriers at Hambledon and the Wood Pigeon at Witley station.

WORMLEY AND CHIDDINGFOLD

The delightful village of Chiddingfold

This is a pleasant walk, mostly on the level, taking us through farmland and woodland. Chiddingfold is a picturesque village with a pond and several seats about a large green.

- **HOW TO GET THERE:** By train to Witley station.
- **PARKING:** At the railway station.
- **LENGTH OF THE WALK:** 6 miles. Map: OS Explorer 133 (GR 948380).

THE WALK

1. We leave the station on the downside and turn right soon to turn left through a stile by a five bar gate, signed 'Lilac Cottage'. At a junction we take the left turn and keeping to this path we cross a drive and go over a stile, across a field and slightly left to a stile and the road. Crossing a stile, almost immediately

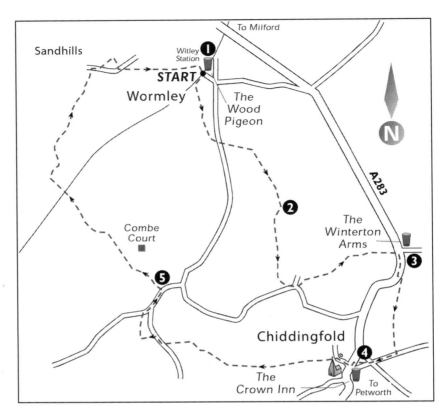

opposite, we shortly enter woods and after some 300 yards we cross another stile. The path goes diagonally across a field to a stile and footbridge and we maintain direction to go over another stile in the corner of the field onto a grassy path.

2. Turning left we soon turn right on a signposted path which bears slightly left away from the hedge, over the brow of the hill and down to a gate and stile visible ahead. We maintain direction for about $\frac{1}{2}$ mile, going over a field, through woodland, along another field and passing behind houses to the road. Turning left we pass a side road and, crossing a grassy bank on our left, we continue on a signposted footpath which soon takes us through trees and over a stile to go across a field. After crossing a stile and footbridge we continue along a grassy path between trees until just before a brick footbridge we turn right on a path soon across fields to a road which we cross.

Refreshments can be found at the Winterton Arms by turning left for 200 yards.

3. Turning right we walk along the road for 300 yards to turn left on a signposted footpath, going over a stile and up a grassy field with the hedge on our left, later through a strip of woodland. We maintain direction with the field edge on our right at first and then across the field and finally out to a road where we turn right, later to reach Chiddingfold village green.

This picturesque centre of Chiddingfold has many old houses round it with the church of St Mary reflected in the village pond. There are several seats to encourage us to linger. The attractive 14th century Crown Inn will provide welcome refreshment. The green has a celebrated annual Bonfire Night on the Saturday nearest to 5th November, which has been held for more than 150 years.

4. Crossing the green we keep the church on our left and the pond on our right. Shortly we turn left on a footpath that takes us up past the churchyard to join a road. As the road turns right, we maintain direction on an enclosed footpath and later through fields finally to go over a stile in the far right hand corner. Continuing on an enclosed path we bear right to cross a drive and a stile. Following the path through the field we negotiate a stile to reach the road where we turn right. Shortly turning left on a signposted footpath we take the first right turn on a footpath which leads us out to a road where we again turn right for a short distance.

5. We turn left through the gate to Combe Court and just after the drive bears right we take a signposted footpath through a kissing gate on our left. Maintaining direction we cross two fields, and go through a wood and another field, eventually crossing the railway. After crossing another field we enter woods, soon to turn right on a bridleway. Crossing a bridge we stay on this bridleway for about $1/2$ mile until we reach the road where we turn right.

Combe Court

At a telephone box we turn left onto Sandhills Common, soon passing a house on the right. At a waymark post, just before a seat, we turn right downhill and finally left, crossing a road to a footpath opposite. After about 600 yards we turn right on a crossing drive back to the station.

Refreshments: Inns at Chiddingfold, and North Bridge (by Witley station).